El Niño & La Niña

Other titles in the *American Disasters* series:

The Challenger Disaster
Tragic Space Flight
ISBN 0-7660-1222-0

The Exxon Valdez
Tragic Oil Spill
ISBN 0-7660-1058-9

Fire in Oakland, California
Billion-Dollar Blaze
ISBN 0-7660-1220-4

The Hindenburg Disaster
Doomed Airship
ISBN 0-7660-1554-8

Hurricane Andrew
Nature's Rage
ISBN 0-7660-1057-0

Love Canal
Toxic Waste Tragedy
ISBN 0-7660-1553-X

Mount St. Helens Volcano
Violent Eruption
ISBN 0-7660-1552-1

The Oklahoma City Bombing
Terror in the Heartland
ISBN 0-7660-1061-9

Polio Epidemic
Crippling Virus Outbreak
ISBN 0-7660-1555-6

Three Mile Island
Nuclear Disaster
ISBN 0-7660-1556-4

The Titanic
Disaster at Sea
ISBN 0-7660-1557-2

Tsunami
Monster Waves
ISBN 0-7660-1786-9

The Siege at Waco
Deadly Inferno
ISBN 0-7660-1218-2

The World Trade Center Bombing
Terror in the Towers
ISBN 0-7660-1056-2

El Niño & La Niña

Deadly Weather

Carmen Bredeson

Enslow Publishers, Inc.

40 Industrial Road
Box 398
Berkeley Heights, NJ 07922
USA

PO Box 38
Aldershot
Hants GU12 6BP
UK

http://www.enslow.com

Library of Congress Cataloging-in-Publication Data

Bredeson, Carmen.
El Nino & La Nina : deadly weather / Carmen Bredeson.
p. cm. — (American disasters)
Includes bibliographical references and index.
ISBN 0-7660-1551-3
1. El Niäno Current—Juvenile literature. 2. Climatic changes—Juvenile literature. [1. El Niäno Current.] I. Title. II.Series.
GC296.8.E4 B74 2001
551.55'0973—dc21
00-011128

Printed in the United States of America

10 9 8 7 6 5 4 3 2 1

To Our Readers:
We have done our best to make sure all Internet addresses in this book were active and appropriate when we went to press. However, the author and the publisher have no control over and assume no liability for the material available on those Internet sites or on other Web sites they may link to. Any comments or suggestions can be sent by e-mail to comments@enslow.com or to the address on the back cover.

Illustration Credits: AP/Wide World Photos, pp. 1, 6, 9, 11, 14, 15, 16, 17, 20, 22, 26, 27, 28, 29, 31, 32, 33, 36, 38; NASA/JPL/Caltech, pp. 39, 40; National Oceanic and Atmospheric Administration (NOAA)/Department of Commerce, p. 23.

Cover Illustration: AP/Wide World Photos.

Contents

Ponderosa Park resident Betty Vorreiter clutches a stuffed animal in the aftermath of a tornado that struck the area on February 22, 1998.

CHAPTER 1

Florida's Deadly Tornadoes

On Sunday, February 22, 1998, people in central Florida were enjoying a beautiful, sunny day. Twelve-year-old Eddie Silva was at a school near his home in Kissimmee, playing basketball with a group of friends. "It was perfect outside," said Silva.[1] Those who lived at nearby Ponderosa Park thought so, too. Many of the people who were camped at the park sat outside, visiting with their neighbors. As darkness fell, people said goodnight and went inside. One by one, the lights blinked off in Kissimmee.

Reg and Hilda Crowe were in their trailer at Ponderosa Park. The Crowes were spending the winter in Florida to escape the cold in Grand Bend, Ontario, their permanent home. Hilda said, "There was a beautiful breeze. Then I heard a whoosh. It sounded like a train getting louder and louder. It lasted a minute, but it seemed like an hour."[2] When their trailer stopped shaking, the Crowes went outside to see what had happened.

One of their neighbors was looking frantically for help. The man's wife and two small children were trapped in their wrecked travel trailer. The Crowes ran to the pile of rubble and helped throw debris aside. Before long, they spotted the woman and her babies. Reg Crowe said, "She had her arms wrapped around the two children. So I found a flashlight and helped get them out."[3] Thankfully, all three were alive.

Two miles from Ponderosa Park, fourteen-year-old Helen Holguin said she had been asleep, but "woke up when I saw lightning. I got up close to the window. When I turned around, everything was on the floor. There was no roof or anything. I started screaming for my little sister. The wind blew me to the floor. I was trembling."[4] Although the house was heavily damaged, Helen and six members of her family survived the deadly tornado that struck their home.

Roaring twisters snaked down from the sky all over central Florida. Eighteen-month-old Jonathan Waldick was asleep in his crib, wrapped in a blanket. When a tornado swept through his house in Kissimmee, it sucked Jonathan out of bed and carried him away. Jonathan's great-grandmother, Shirley Driver, ran to his room but could not find the baby in the wreckage.

Driver ran outside and started looking around the yard for Jonathan. Neighbors joined in the search and sifted through piles of rubble left behind by the twister. After about thirty minutes of searching, someone spotted a tiny foot sticking out of a pile of tree limbs and debris.

The tornadoes that struck Florida on February 22, 1998, were among the most destructive in the state's history.

Fearing the worst, Driver and her neighbors quickly uncovered Jonathan. Much to their joy, they found the baby alive and still wrapped in his blanket. Other than a few scratches, Jonathan was not hurt. Shirley Driver's house was destroyed, but she said, "I don't care about this as long as he's here."[5]

In Sanford, Florida, Julie and David Myers and their six-year-old daughter Brittany were asleep when the tornado took aim at their house. Brittany called out for her mother as the tornado hit. Julie Myers said, "We had no time. I got to her and laid down over her just as the windows blew out."[6] The house collapsed around the terrified family. They survived, but many of their neighbors did not.

In Daytona Beach, Florida, Mark Price and his fiancée, Jennifer Johnson, woke up to the roar of an approaching tornado. As the wind began to shake their trailer, Price shoved Johnson into a small closet. She grabbed his hand to pull him into the closet with her. The tornado hit and Johnson felt Price's hand slipping away. Mark Price's body was found later just a few feet from his home. Jennifer Johnson sadly remembered, "One minute I was holding his hand, and then he was gone."[7]

The February 22 tornadoes were the most deadly in Florida's history. Central Florida, especially areas in and around Kissimmee, were hit hardest. At least three lines of twisters bore down on the area early in the morning. Wind speeds inside the tornadoes may have reached as high as 210 miles per hour.

On the morning after the deadly twisters, scattered heaps of rubble were found everywhere. Eddie Silva, who had been playing basketball just hours before, said, "Everything is totally different. It looks like a dumpster."[8] The ground was covered with pieces of twisted metal and piles of pink insulation, splintered wood, clothes, books, toys, and pictures. Peoples' homes and possessions had been ripped apart and left in heaps.

Rescue teams began arriving at daylight, searching for

A Kissimmee resident takes a break from sifting through the rubble left in the wake of the deadly tornadoes. At least eight hundred homes were completely destroyed.

survivors in and around broken homes. Police K-9 units used their trained dogs to locate victims trapped in the rubble. Sometimes, the rescue teams were too late. Forty-two people were killed during the terrible February twisters in Florida. At least eight hundred homes were destroyed and hundreds more were damaged.

CHAPTER 2

California's Killer Floods

While the residents of Florida were cleaning up from the tornadoes, Californians were being pounded with rain. February 1998 was shaping up to be one of the wettest months on record in the state. For weeks, rain had been falling along the California coast. At first, the dry ground soaked up the moisture like a sponge. Soon, though, the ground became saturated and could not hold any more water. Rivers of mud ran down the sides of hills. Swollen streams spilled out of their banks.

At 2:30 A.M. on the morning of February 24, California Highway Patrol officers Britt Irvine and Rich Stovall were headed toward Highway 166, northwest of Santa Barbara. A truck driver was stranded and needed help. The officers did not know that a section of Highway 166 over the Cuyama River had washed out. Fog in the area made it hard to see anything. As the police cruiser sped along, the road suddenly disappeared. All of a sudden the car was in

Many California roads and highways were badly damaged by heavy rains in February 1998. This 600-foot-long sinkhole across Balboa Avenue in San Diego was the result of a burst storm drain.

the air! It flipped over and plunged fifteen feet into the raging Cuyama River.

At around the same time, Steve Miller was also driving on Highway 166. Miller said, "By the time I saw the fog, I was airborne."[1] His car landed in the river and Miller struggled to get out of the passenger door. He escaped just as the car started floating away. Miller swam through the swiftly flowing water and pulled himself onto shore. There he sat, wet and shivering, hoping someone would rescue him before the swollen river rose any higher.

Back at Highway Patrol headquarters, the police dispatcher was wondering why officers Stovall and Irvine had not checked in. The dispatcher tried to contact the police cruiser over and over. His attempts failed and a Santa Barbara sheriff's deputy was sent to investigate. When the deputy got to the washed-out highway, he was barely able to stop his car before it plunged into the river. The cruiser's front wheels were suspended in air over the water when the deputy clambered out of the car.

By the time help arrived, six cars and a tractor-trailer rig had gone over the edge and been carried away by the river. A helicopter search team spotted Steve Miller and plucked him from the riverbank three hours after his car had sunk into the muddy water.

When rescue teams reached the police cruiser, they found it buried upside down in a sandbank. Officers Rich Stovall and Britt Irvine had been trapped in the car and drowned. Two other motorists also lost their lives in the Cuyama River on the night of February 24. In all, nine people died during the late February storms that struck California in 1998.

The view from within the huge sinkhole on San Diego's Balboa Avenue in March 1998.

Gary Lemonoff of Laguna Beach, California, remembers

The remains of several California homes are shown dangling on the edge of a cliff. Many houses were knocked off their foundations by the flooding rain and mudslides.

a terrible night in February when a huge mudflow swept past his home. "I'll never forget in my life the noise I heard. There was a roar, my trailer started shaking, and rocks and mud and boulders and tree limbs went rolling across my driveway."[2] Lemonoff could hear his neighbors screaming for help in the blackness of the night.

Another Laguna Beach resident, seventy-four-year-old Eldon Setterholm, said, "All of a sudden everyone started yelling, 'Get out! Get out! The mountain is coming down!' I ended up doing the breast stroke in the mud."[3] Many California houses were pushed off of their foundations by rivers of rain and mud.

Seventy-five-year-old Beverly Axelrod loved her home in Pacifica. "It was just wonderful to live by the ocean . . . I could not see anything but the ocean from every room in my house. I felt like I was all alone on a ship. Sea birds, dolphins, glorious sunsets," said Axelrod.[4]

On February 22, Axelrod picked up a friend at the

Firemen cut a house in half on February 25, 1998, in Pacifica, California. The house sat on a cliff that was made unstable by the high surf and heavy rains. If it had not been cut in half, the entire house would have fallen off the cliff.

airport. When they got home, a police officer was knocking on the front door of Axelrod's house. The officer said it was time to evacuate because the house was starting to slide down the hill. If allowed to stand, it might crash into the house below it. The house would need to be demolished immediately. Beverly Axelrod spent the day moving her things out of the doomed house. She returned the next day to see it being destroyed. "I watched them as they cut it in half. It was like cutting through my own heart."[5]

In February of 1998, people all over California were coping with huge amounts of rain, flash floods, mudslides, and hurricane-force winds. Usually, only a small amount of rain falls during the month of February. In 1998, the normally gentle rains turned into downpours. Torrents of water broke sewage systems. Near the Los Angeles and Ventura County Line, 16 million gallons of raw sewage poured out of storm drains and into the ocean. Beaches were closed for miles because of the spill.

What was causing the terrible weather in California and Florida? Meteorologists blamed an area of warmer-than-normal water in the tropical Pacific, called El Niño. How could something as simple as warm water, far away in the Tropics, be responsible for such devastation?

CHAPTER 3

What is El Niño?

El Niño can be compared to a big hot tub full of warm water. In the Pacific Ocean, the water near the equator gets very warm because the sunlight is so strong. In most years, trade winds blowing from east to west across the ocean push the warm water toward the western Pacific and away from South America.

Once the warm water is gone, cooler water rises to the surface along the west coast of South America. The cooler water is full of plankton. Plankton are very small animals and plants that live in seas and lakes. Fish and sea creatures swim in the cool water and eat the plentiful plankton, which provide them with important nutrients.

During an El Niño event, the trade winds get weaker and can blow the opposite direction. This moves the pool of warm water toward South America instead of away from it. Areas of the Pacific Ocean where the water is normally cool have warm water instead. There are not as many plankton in warm water, so fish leave the area.

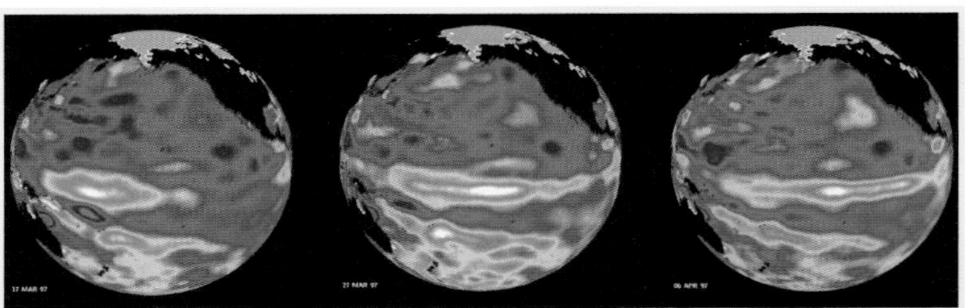

The red and white portions of this satellite image of the earth show where a warm water mass existed in May 1997. This provided scientists with strong evidence that El Niño was on its way.

Marine biologist Tom Okey explained, "Not only are there fewer nutrients, but warm water doesn't hold nutrients as effectively as cold water. The whole ecosystem suffers."[1]

Small fish called anchovies are a very important catch for the fishing industry in Peru. The country of Peru is located on the west coast of South America. Long ago, the Peruvian fishermen noticed that every few years, water off the coast got very warm. When this happened, the anchovies were driven north to find food in cooler water. With the anchovies gone, the fishing business in Peru suffered.

Because the periodic warming of the water in the eastern Pacific usually happened around Christmas time, fishermen named these periods El Niño de Navidad, which means the Christ child. This name was eventually shortened to El Niño, which means the boy child.

In addition to sending the anchovies north, El Niño also has a big effect on weather patterns all over the globe.

National Weather Service Climate Analysis Center director David Rodenhuis explains that, "Apart from the change of seasons, El Niño is the most important recurring event affecting world climates."[2]

Because two thirds of the earth is covered with water, temperature changes in the oceans make a big impact on the weather. Warm ocean water heats up the air above it. Warmer air produces more clouds and more rain. Cool ocean water cools off the air above it. Cooler air produces fewer clouds and less rain.

During an El Niño event, the huge pool of warm water in the western Pacific Ocean heats up the air above it. This air rises, adds moisture to the atmosphere, and changes the pattern of the jet stream. The jet stream is a fast-moving flow of air in the upper atmosphere. The jet stream carries weather systems to all parts of the earth. When it is disrupted, or changed, the typical weather of an area is also changed.

During the 1997–1998 El Niño, the warmer-than-normal pool of water in the Pacific Ocean was nearly twice as large as the continental United States. This huge pool of warm water disrupted weather patterns and brought floods, tornadoes, forest fires, and droughts to various places on earth.

The last big El Niño before the one in 1997–1998 occurred in 1982–1983. It had been called the strongest El Niño of the twentieth century. Peru was flooded with eleven feet of rain. Australia and parts of Africa suffered

Children in Peru carry buckets of water in an effort to clean their flooded homes in March 1998. Fishermen in Peru were responsible for naming the El Niño weather phenomenon.

severe droughts. California was hit with heavy rain and huge waves.

The 1982–1983 El Niño caught scientists by surprise. At that time, there were only about a dozen weather buoys in the Pacific Ocean. The floating buoys are small weather stations that keep track of conditions at each location. The need for more information led to the Tropical Atmosphere Ocean Array Project (TAO), which was completed in 1994. TAO weather buoys were anchored in seventy locations in the tropical Pacific Ocean. The buoys gave scientists a way to study the ocean temperatures and predict when an El Niño might occur.

Instruments on the buoys measure the surface water temperature along with the subsurface water temperature down to sixteen hundred feet. Air temperature, wind speed, and humidity are also measured constantly. Data from the buoys is beamed up to orbiting satellites. A satellite is a natural or man-made object that orbits a larger body in space. The satellites send the data back down to the Pacific Marine Environmental Laboratory in Seattle, Washington. The laboratory is part of the United States National Oceanic and Atmospheric Administration

An NOAA scientist services one of the buoys of the Pacific array. These buoys help warn us of upcoming El Niño events by tracking ocean temperatures.

(NOAA). Scientists process the data and use it to make weather predictions.

The TOPEX/Poseidon satellite, which was launched in 1992, also provides data for weather forecasters. The satellite is a joint project between the United States and France. TOPEX/Poseidon orbits 830 miles above earth's surface. A radar beam is sent from the satellite to the ocean below. The beam is reflected off of the ocean and returned to the satellite. The data is then relayed to NASA's Jet Propulsion Laboratory (JPL) in Pasadena, California. The amount of time it takes the beam to return to TOPEX/Poseidon from the ocean shows scientists the height of the ocean surface.

The data from both TAO and TOPEX/Poseidon made it possible for scientists to predict an El Niño event for the first time in 1997. NASA oceanographer William Patzert explained, "This is the first time we saw it right from the beginning."[3] Scientists watched as El Niño grew larger and larger and began disrupting weather patterns all over the earth.

CHAPTER 4

El Niño Worldwide

It is hard to say exactly how much damage to life and property occurred as a direct result of the 1997–1998 El Niño. We do know that El Niño impacted weather patterns across the whole world, with both good and bad results.

Droughts caused by El Niño contributed to forest fires in Australia, the Philippines, Indonesia, and Mexico. Fires in central and northern Mexico were first reported in December 1997. By April 1998, an estimated nine thousand individual fires burned out of control. Millions of acres of timber went up in smoke. The fires were hard to fight because they were in remote locations that firefighters could not reach. Smoke from the fires drifted north and covered much of Texas with a sooty haze.

Texas Governor George W. Bush responded to the crisis by warning that, "Texas is in a very serious situation when it comes to the quality of air. It's very important for the people of the state of Texas to take precautions.

Portions of the Amazon forest burn in March 1998. Droughts caused by El Niño helped such fires spread more quickly and also made them difficult to put out.

Don't exercise outside, stay indoors and be reasonable in how you conduct your daily life."[1] Health alerts were issued in many Texas towns. The smoky haze covering Texas also spread into Oklahoma, Colorado, and as far away as Wisconsin.

Fires affected the quality of the air in Texas in May 1998. George W. Bush, then the governor of Texas, responded to the crisis by issuing a warning to citizens of the state.

Too much rain, instead of too little, was a deadly problem in parts of Peru. Several feet of rain fell on areas of Peru that normally received only inches each year. Dozens of bridges and roads were washed out and many people died in the floods. In the town of Chato Chico, the Piura River spilled out of its banks on February 15, 1998. Torrents of muddy water swept into homes along the river. Soon, the water was chest deep. According to Isaias Silva, the raging water "took all the little animals. Then my house just fell down completely."[2]

Sixty miles south of Chato Chico, the village of Motse was also overtaken by rising water. Manuel Guevara Sanchez said that residents "strung ropes from one house

Rescue workers in Ecuador search for mudslide victims in April 1998.

to another to rescue people. Some spent three days on the roof. Those who knew how to swim brought them food."[3] When the floodwaters receded, ten villagers were found dead.

In Equador, a landslide caused by the wet ground broke a large oil pipeline. The resulting explosion killed seventeen people and burned seventy-four more. Worldwide, more than two thousand people died in El Niño-related weather disasters. An estimated $33 billion in damage was caused by the pool of warm ocean water in the Tropics.[4]

Wildlife was also affected by the changing weather patterns. On the Indonesian island of Borneo, there were months of forest fires and drought. Orangutans, red-haired apes, were dying of starvation on the island. Orangutans are considered endangered, which means they are in danger of becoming extinct—disappearing altogether. Willie Smits, head of the Wanariset Samboja Primate Refuge in Borneo, explained, "The jungle is black and bare. There is no fruit, no leaves, no bark. There's nothing for them to eat, no water to drink. Babies are too

On the island of Borneo, an orangutan is seen eating a banana while a fire burns in the distance.

weak to cling to their mothers. They are falling out of the trees and are left to die."[5]

Off the coast of California, many seals and sea lions were also in trouble. Violent storms sent powerful waves crashing onto the rocky islands where they lived. Hundreds of these animals were injured or killed by the storms. In addition, the food the animals usually ate was in short supply because of the warm water. Many species of fish had gone north in search of cooler water.

At the Mammal Care Center in San Pedro, California, Jackie Ott and her small staff tried to nurse some of the injured and starving sea lions and seals back to health. According to Ott, "There are thousands of sea lion pups who've been separated from their mothers and are dying. We think there is going to be a 90 percent mortality rate [off the West Coast] for pups this year."[6]

In the too-warm eastern Pacific, the food chain depends on cool water moving from the deep ocean to the surface, bringing nutrients with it. The warm water associated with El Niño had stopped the normal movement of cool water. Millions of sea creatures, fish, and birds could not find food and starved to death.

Not all creatures suffered as a result of El Niño. In desert regions of the American Southwest, heavy rains caused many more plants to grow than was normal. More plants meant more food for animals. There was a large increase in the number of deer mice in the area because of the extra food. These rodents carry a disease called hantavirus, which can be a deadly threat to people who

Starving sea lion pups are fed at the Friends of the Sea Lion Marine Mammal Center in Laguna Beach, California, in December of 1997. Many sea lions faced starvation as a result of El Niño's effect on their food supply.

Grasshoppers thrived on the El Niño weather and overran many towns in California.

catch it. Flooded regions of the world were also perfect breeding grounds for mosquitoes, which can spread diseases such as malaria to people.

Some insects were not necessarily a health threat, but were certainly a nuisance. In California, several towns were overrun by millions of grasshoppers. Too much rain had sent the insects from the countryside into towns. People swept grasshoppers out of their houses and stores. Grasshoppers even got into schools and buzzed the students in hallways and classrooms.

Still others benefited from the effects of El Niño. Surfers flocked to the coast of California to take advantage of the enormous waves that came crashing ashore. One surfer said, "It teaches you a new appreciation for the ocean. Shows you how bad Mother Nature is. Even at night you lay back and listen to the tide rush, each wave crashing. It's beautiful!"[7] The water was so warm that surfers did not have to wear wet suits. Wet suits are rubber outfits that keep the swimmer's body warm in cold water.

Some fishermen also had a real treat in store. Fish that usually lived further south were driven north. Barracuda

California surfers enjoyed riding the high waves caused by El Niño in January of 1998.

and tuna were caught in Santa Monica Bay, and marlin were found as far north as Oregon.

Flowers also bloomed in areas where cactus was usually the only thing growing. In the mountains near Tucson, Arizona, extra rain brought a dense carpet of wildflowers to the region. Flowers also bloomed in profusion all over Death Valley, California. This desert is normally the driest and hottest place in North America and almost never sees such growth.

NASA oceanographer Michael McPhaden reported, "There were blockbuster impacts all over the world. This El Niño is going to be a benchmark for years to come."[8]

The 1982–1983 El Niño could no longer be called the strongest El Niño of the century. "We didn't even know that one was happening until it was almost over," continued McPhaden. "In the 1997–1998 El Niño, we could tell you day by day what was happening."[9]

CHAPTER 5

Studying the Weather

Even with all of the information available, scientists still do not know what causes an El Niño to begin or end. By April 1998, the powerful El Niño that had caused so much misery during the previous year was fading away. National Weather Service meteorologist Vernon Kousky said, "El Niño is beginning to taper down. We are starting that gradual process of a return to normal."[1] JPL's William Patzert agreed when he said, "The volume of the warm pool has thinned to near-normal conditions. It has really run its full course."[2]

The giant warm pool of water in the western Pacific was gradually cooling and shrinking. Another El Niño event was nearly over. There have been twenty-three El Niños during the past ninety-eight years, according to NOAA.[3] The four most powerful El Niños in that time-frame have occurred since 1980.

As the 1997–1998 El Niño slowly weakened, scientists began looking for signs of another weather pattern

A rescue worker searches for survivors in the remains of a flooded home in Ecuador in April 1998. By this time, El Niño was already winding down and scientists were waiting for signs of La Niña to begin.

known as La Niña, which means the girl child. La Niña is often called El Niño's little sister. Fifteen of the last twenty-three El Niños have been followed by a La Niña.

During a La Niña event, conditions are usually the opposite of ones seen during an El Niño. Parts of the world that were plagued by too much rain during an El Niño often suffer droughts during a La Niña. William Patzert explains that "La Niña is El Niño upside-down. The warm pool becomes the cool pool . . . The impact is the reverse of El Niño."[4]

By June 1998, conditions in the tropical Pacific started to point to a La Niña event. The warm surface water in the

Pacific was being pushed toward Asia. La Niña brings east winds that are stronger than normal. They push the warm water toward Asia and away from South America. Cooler than normal water along the west coast of South America cools the air above it. Cooler air results in fewer clouds and less rain. Areas that got too much rain during El Niño, such as Peru and California, experienced drier conditions while La Niña dominated the Pacific Ocean. Also, places that were dry during El Niño, such as parts of India, Australia, and Africa, had more rain during La Niña.

The cool pool of water in the tropical Pacific that is present during La Niña lasted from spring 1998 until spring 2000. In June 2000, TOPEX/Poseidon data showed that the cool La Niña water was getting warmer. After a year of an extra-large El Niño followed by two years of La Niña, weather patterns in the tropical Pacific finally began returning to normal.

Weather scientists have some new tools to help them follow weather patterns such as El Niño and La Niña. The QuikScat satellite was launched in 1999. It gives a daily picture of the winds that swirl above the oceans of the world. QuikScat is also able to track changes in the trade winds that blow along the equator.

NASA's Dr. Ghassem Asrar reports that, "Knowledge about which way the wind blows and how hard it is blowing may seem simple, but this kind of information is actually a critical tool in improved weather forecasting, early storm detection and identifying subtle changes in global climate."[5]

Benjamin Franklin was very interested in predicting the weather. He observed that large storms usually moved from west to east across the U.S.

The Terra satellite, which was also launched in 1999, is another part of NASA's Earth Science Enterprise. It provides information each day about the earth's oceans, atmosphere, life, lands, and clouds and how they influence each other. Terra Project scientist Dr. Yoram Kaufman said, "The data will help us understand our planet, aid in our distinguishing between natural and human-induced changes, and show us how the earth's climate affects the quality of our lives."[6]

Benjamin Franklin was the first American to recognize the value of predicting weather. While reading newspaper articles about severe weather, he concluded that large storm systems usually move from west to east across the United States. He thought it would be helpful if people could be notified ahead of time of approaching storms. At that time, there was no fast way to contact people across the country.

After the telegraph was invented in 1837, it became

An artist's conception of the TOPEX/Poseidon satellite. First launched in 1992, the satellite collects data on the world's oceans.

possible to link all parts of the United States. Weather watchers sent their reports along telegraph lines to a central office. For the first time, a weather map was created which showed the movement of storms across America. Information was sent to towns in the path of severe storms.

However, storms over the oceans were still unpredictable. The oceans were too big for people to see what kind of weather was forming over them. Weather balloons and airplanes were able to fly overhead and take pictures,

An artist's conception of the Jason-1 satellite, scheduled for launch in September 2001.

but they could only provide a brief look at conditions. What scientists needed was an "eye in the sky" that could continuously monitor the earth.

The first weather "eye," TIROS 1, was launched into orbit by NASA on April 1, 1960. The 270-pound satellite had two cameras that sent back thousands of fuzzy black and white pictures of the cloud tops surrounding the earth. It gave scientists their first look at our planet from space.

Dozens of weather satellites have been put into orbit around earth since 1960. Today's satellites do much more than photograph the clouds. Satellites like the TOPEX/Poseidon measure the height of the oceans, take temperatures all over the earth, track plankton in the ocean, and even watch volcanoes erupt. These satellites also watch cold fronts move across the continents and snap pictures of hurricanes and typhoons as they form.

The TOPEX/Poseidon project is operated jointly by NASA and the French Space Agency, Centre National d'Etudes Satiales (CNES). The project's three-year prime mission ended in the fall of 1995 and it is now in its extended observational phase. A follow-up mission called Jason-1 is scheduled for launch in September 2001. The Jason-1 satellite will monitor global ocean circulation and will continue to help predict future El Niño events.

Satellites are always in the sky, scanning the globe day and night. When another El Niño begins to form, weather forecasters will be the first to know.

Other Famous Storms

DATE	PLACE	STORM	CASUALTIES
September 8, 1900	Galveston, Texas	Hurricane	6,000 dead from winds and tidal wave.
June 14, 1903	Hippner, Oregon	Flood	325 dead.
June 25–30, 1957	Texas to Alabama	Hurricane Audrey	390 dead.
September 7–12, 1965	Mississippi and Louisiana	Hurricane Betsy	74 dead.
January 18–26, 1969	Southern California	Floods and mudslides	100 dead.
August 17–19, 1969	Mississippi and Louisiana	Hurricane Camille	256 dead.
July 31, 1976	Colorado	Flood on Big Thompson River	139 dead.
August 23–26, 1992	Florida and Louisiana	Hurricane Andrew	26 dead.
March 12–14, 1993	Eastern United States	Blizzard	270 estimated dead.
Summer 1993	Midwest United States	Floods from torrential rains	51 dead.

Chapter Notes

Chapter 1. Florida's Deadly Tornadoes

1. Joseph Duarte, "Twisters Take Deadly Toll," *Houston Chronicle*, February 24, 1998, p. A11.

2. Tom Fennell, "The Rage of El Niño," *MacLean's*, March 9, 1998, p. 35.

3. Ibid., p. 35.

4. Duarte, p. A11.

5. Christopher John Farley, "Twisters, Tragedies and Miracles," *Time*, March 9, 1998, p. 73.

6. Kim Cobb, "Landscape Paints a Tale of Terror," *Houston Chronicle*, February 24, 1998, p. A1.

7. Fennell, p. 34.

8. Duarte, p. A11.

Chapter 2. California's Killer Floods

1. Todd Purdum, "At Least 7 Die In Worst of El Niño Storms," *Houston Chronicle*, 2-Star Edition, February 25, 1998, p. A10.

2. J. Madeline Nash, "A State of Instability," *Time*, March 9, 1998, p. 72.

3. Stephanie Simon, "At Least 6 Die in Latest of El Niño Storms," *Houston Chronicle*, 3-Star Edition, February 25, 1998, p. A10.

4. Michael McCabe, "El Niño's Gone, Nightmare Lingers," *San Francisco Chronicle*, March 12, 1999, p. 1.

5. Ibid.

Chapter 3. What is El Niño?

1. Douglas Gantenbein, "El Niño's Other Costs," *Audubon*, January/February 1998, p. 16.

2. Ronald Wagner and Bill Adler, *The Weather Sourcebook* (Old Saybrook, Conn.: The Globe Pequot Press, 1994), p. 81.

3. Jason Starr, "Eye on the Ocean," <http://earthobservatory.nasa.gov/Study/EyeOcean/> (March 1, 2000).

Chapter 4. El Niño Worldwide

1. Polly Ross Hughes, "U.S. Experts Go to Mexico as Hazealert Issued for All of Texas," *Houston Chronicle*, May 16, 1998, p. A1.

2. Curt Suplee, "El Niño/La Niña," *National Geographic*, March 1999, p. 76.

3. Ibid., p. 77.

4. Ibid., p. 73.

5. "Borneo's Wildfires May Push Its Orangutans Into Extinction," *Houston Chronicle*, April 9, 1998, p. A20.

6. Michael Neill, "Back in the Swim," *People*, March 16, 1998, p. 115.

7. Henry Porter, *Forecast: Disaster* (New York: Dell Publishing, 1999), p. 87.

8. Douglas Gantenbein, "Forecast For El Niño," *Popular Science*, August 1998, p. 59.

9. Ibid., p. 60.

Chapter 5. Studying the Weather

1. Brian Meehan, "It's Evident El Niño's Fading," *Houston Chronicle*, May 11, 1998, p. 6-Discovery.

2. Ibid.

3. Curt Suplee, "El Niño/La Niña," *National Geographic*, March 1999, p. 94.

4. Meehan, p.6-Discovery.

5. "El Niño Watcher Blasts Off," n.d., <http://www.ssl.msfc.nasa.gov/newhome/headlines/essd20jun991.htm> (May 2, 2000).

6. "Terra Spacecraft Open For Business," Jet Propulsion Laboratory Media Relations Office, April 19, 2000. <http://terra.nasa.gov/Events/FirstImages/> (May 2, 2000).

Glossary

atmosphere—The gaseous envelope that surrounds earth.

buoy—A floating object anchored in a body of water.

climate—Average weather conditions for a place.

drought—A long period of dry weather conditions.

ecosystem—Plants, animals, and microscopic life that live together in an area.

equator—An imaginary circle around the middle of the earth.

evacuate—To leave a place for safety reasons.

jet stream—Bands of high moving winds moving from west to east around the earth.

meteorologist—A scientist who studies the earth's atmosphere and weather.

nutrient—A part of a food that promotes health and growth.

oceanographer—A scientist who studies oceans and the living things in them.

plankton—Microscopic animal and plant life found in seas and lakes.

satellite—A man-made device created to orbit a planet or moon.

trade winds—A wind that blows toward the equator.

Further Reading

Arnold, Caroline. *El Niño.* New York: Clarion Books, 1998.

Elsom, Derek M. *Weather Explained.* New York: Henry Holt, 1997.

Fagan, Brian. Floods, *Famines & Emperors: El Niño & the Fate of Civilizations.* New York: Basic Books, 1999.

Gardner, Robert and Webster, David. *Science Projects About Weather.* Berkeley Heights, NJ: Enslow, 1994.

Gold, Susan Dudley. *Blame It on El Niño.* Austin, TX: Steck-Vaughn, 2000.

Herman, Gail. *Storm Chasers.* New York: Grossett & Dunlap, 1997.

Seibert, Patricia. *Discovering El Niño: How Fable & Fact Together Help Explain the Weather.* Brookfield, CT: Millbrook Press, 1999.

Suplee, Curt. "El Niño/La Niña." *National Geographic,* March 1999.

Internet Addresses

TOPEX/Poseidon Mission Page
http://topex-www.jpl.nasa.gov

Earth Observatory: Eye on the Ocean
http://earthobservatory.nasa.gov/Study/EyeOcean/

Climate Prediction Center
http://www.cpc.ncep.noaa.gov/

TIROS 40th Anniversary
http://pao.gsfc.nasa.gov/gsfc/earth/tiros/tiros.htm

Tropical Atmosphere Ocean (TAO) Project Home Page
http://www.pmel.noaa.gov/tao/index.shtml

Index